CONNECTICUT
The Constitution State

TEN TOP FACTS ABOUT CONNECTICUT

★ ★ ★ ★ ★ ★ ★ ★ ★ ★ ★ ★ ★

•State nicknames:	The Constitution State, The Nutmeg State
•State motto:	*Qui Transtulit Sustinet* ("He who transplanted still sustains")
•Capital:	Hartford
•Area:	5,006 square miles
•State flower:	Mountain laurel
•State tree:	White oak
•State bird:	American robin
•State insect:	Praying mantis
•State shellfish:	Eastern oyster
•State song:	"Yankee Doodle"

To Lily and Ethan, and those wonderful Connecticut natives, Paula, Peter, Nathaniel, and Lizzie.

p. 4: U.S. Mint; p. 5: (top right) Brown Brothers, Sterling, PA, (bottom left) Bettmann/Corbis, New York, NY; p. 6: (top right) Bettmann/Corbis, (bottom) North Wind Picture Archives, Alfred, ME; p. 7: Brown Brothers; p. 8: (top right) Bettmann/Corbis, (bottom) Brown Brothers; p. 9: (top) Brown Brothers, (bottom left and right) North Wind Picture Archives; p. 10: Connecticut Historical Society; p. 11: (top) Bettmann/Corbis, (bottom) Underwood & Underwood/Corbis; p. 12: (top) Bettmann/Corbis, (bottom) Mystic Seaport/S. Fisher, Mystic, CT; p. 13: Bettmann/Corbis; p. 14: Brown Brothers; p. 15: Corbis; p. 16: (top left) P. Schermeister/Corbis, (bottom right) J. McElholm/Greater Hartford Tourism District; p. 17: P. Schermeister/Corbis; p. 18: (top left) Dinosaur State Park, Rocky Hill, CT, (bottom left) J. Marshall/Corbis, (right) L. Snider/Corbis; p. 19: (top left) J. Muldoon/Connecticut Office of Tourism, (top right) L. Snider/Corbis, (bottom right) J. McElholm/Greater Hartford Tourism District; p. 20: (left) Robert Benson Photography, Old State House, Hartford, CT, (top right) Corbis, (bottom right) The Barnum Museum, Bridgeport, CT; p. 21: (top left) Holahan/Mashantucket Pequot Museum, Mashantucket, CT, (bottom left) L. Snider/Corbis, (right) Yogi, Inc./Corbis; p. 22: Brown Brothers (Barnum), Scholastic Photo Archives (Brown), Pacha-(Pacha)/Corbis (Close), Library of Congress (Grasso); p. 23: Brown Brothers (Hale), Brown Brothers (Hepburn), Bettmann/Corbis (Ives), AP/World Wide Photos (Nader), The National Park Service (Olmstead); p. 24: Gale Research, Detroit, MI (O'Neill), North Wind Picture Archives (Stowe), Scholastic Photo Archives (Webster and Whitney); p. 25: North Wind Picture Archives.

Photo research by Dwayne Howard

All other illustrations by John Speirs

ISBN 0-439-22214-1

12 11 10 9 8 7 6 5 4 3 2 1   1 2 3 4 5/0

Designed by Madalina Stefan

Printed in the U.S.A.

First Scholastic printing, January 2001

CONNECTICUT
The Constitution State

By S. A. Kitzen

SCHOLASTIC INC.

New York   Toronto   London   Auckland   Sydney   Mexico City   New Delhi   Hong Kong

A Celebration of the Fifty States

★ ★ ★ ★ ★ ★ ★ ★ ★ ★ ★ ★

In January 1999, the U.S. Mint started an ambitious ten-year program to commemorate each of the fifty United States. Over the next several years (through 2008), they will issue five newly designed quarters each year.

One side (obverse) of each new quarter will display the profile of George Washington and the words *Liberty, In God We Trust,* and *United States of America.* The other side (reverse) will feature a design honoring a specific state's unique history, the year it became a state, the year of the quarter's issue, and the words *E Pluribus Unum* (Latin for "from many, one"). The quarters are being issued in the order in which the states joined the union, beginning with the thirteen original colonies.

To find out more about the 50 State Quarters™ Program, visit the official U.S. Mint Web site at *www.usmint.gov.*

CONNECTICUT'S QUARTER: Disappearing Act

In 1662, King Charles II of England granted a charter to the colony of Connecticut that made it nearly independent from England. All the other colonies at the time were ruled by officials appointed by the king, but Connecticut was allowed to elect its own governor.

For twenty-five years, Connecticut thrived and its inhabitants lived peacefully side by side with the surrounding colonies. Then, in October 1687, Sir Edmund Andros, governor of the Dominion of New England, challenged Connecticut's government and tried to gain control of the colony. When Sir Edmond arrived in Hartford, the capital, he ordered the colonial government to hand over their charter. According to legend, during angry discussions between Sir Edmond and the others, all the candles lighting the room went out. When they were relit, the charter was gone.

Captain Joseph Wadsworth had hidden it in a great white oak tree. This tree came to be known as the Charter Oak, and this famous symbol of strength and independence is depicted on Connecticut's quarter. The actual tree fell during a storm in August 1856.

The First Settlers

Long before the seventeenth century, the land that is now Connecticut was occupied by many Native American tribes, including the Pequot, the Mohawk, and the Mohegan, among others. The state's name comes from an Indian word, *Quinnehukgut,* which means "beside the long tidal river." The first European explorer to set foot in Connecticut was a Dutchman named Adriaen Block. After he discovered the natural riches of the land, he returned with some of his countrymen and began trading with the Indians. In 1633, the Dutch immigrants built the House of Hope, a trading post and fort, and started a small settlement near what is now Hartford.

Thomas Hooker

John Winthrop

At about the same time, several English colonists from Massachusetts traveled south to Connecticut in search of more fertile land and greater political and religious freedom and started new colonies. John Oldham settled Wethersfield, William Holmes settled the colony of Windsor, and John Winthrop established Saybrook. In 1636, the largest group of colonists to migrate from Massachusetts was led by a well-known minister, Thomas Hooker, who started a settlement in Hartford. A separate colony was established in Quinnipiac (now New Haven) by Reverend John Davenport in 1638. The Indians sold

Indians teaching settlers to farm

Reverend John Davenport

land to the colonial settlers and taught them to grow corn and other crops. One tribe in particular resented the presence of the British — the Pequot. In 1637, after John Oldham was killed by the Indians, an armed band of colonists led by Captain John Mason staged a brutal attack on the Pequot. More than six hundred of the Indians died in the attack, nearly wiping out the tribe forever.

John Mason's attack on the Pequot, 1637

The Fundamental Orders

In 1639, leaders from the Hartford, Windsor, and Wethersfield settlements decided to unite and form the Connecticut Colony. Thomas Hooker, the leader of the Hartford colony, met with several other ministers and colonial leaders and wrote a code of laws by which the colony would be governed. This code was called the Fundamental Orders, and it is considered the first constitution ever written. Based on the principle of self-government, it recognized the people's right to vote directly for their officials and to limit the officials' power. The Fundamental Orders helped provide the basis for the U.S. Constitution. That's why Connecticut is nicknamed "The Constitution State."

In 1662, King Charles II granted Connecticut the charter that was later hidden in the Charter Oak for safe-keeping. In 1665, the New Haven and Connecticut colonies united.

The Charter Oak

War!

For nearly a hundred years, Connecticut thrived as a colony, with little involvement by the British. But tension between England and the other colonies mounted until the first shots of the Revolutionary War were fired in 1775. More than 3,000 men from Connecticut fought in the war, including the extraordinary heroes Nathan Hale, Ethan Allen, and Israel Putnam. Nathan Hale served as a spy for General George Washington. Ethan Allen led a famous battle and captured the British Fort Ticonderoga without losing any of his soldiers. Israel Putnam was a fierce patriot who was in command of New York City until George Washington arrived.

Another well-known man from Connecticut, Benedict Arnold, was not a hero of the war, but a traitor. In fact, his

Ethan Allen

Nathan Hale as a spy in the enemy's camp

Fort Ticonderoga

name is now a synonym for the word. He served as a general in the Continental army before moving over to the side of the British. As a British general he led the defeat of the colonists in two terrible battles in 1781 — one at Fort Trumbull in New London, the other at Fort Griswold near the town of Groton.

On July 4, 1776, four delegates from Connecticut attended the Continental Congress in Philadelphia and signed the Declaration of Independence. One of them, a judge named Roger Sherman, helped to write it, too.

Israel Putnam

Benedict Arnold

Soldiers of the Continental army

The Connecticut Compromise

When the British had surrendered and the Revolutionary War was over, once again delegates from the thirteen colonies met in Philadelphia to write a constitution to govern their new nation. The smaller states, Connecticut among them, worried that they would be unfairly represented in Congress because of their size. It took some time, but eventually the colonies agreed that there would be two houses of Congress. The Upper House, the Senate, would be made up of two senators from each state, regardless of its size. The members of the House of Representatives would be elected according to the population of each state. The delegates from Connecticut played a key role in the plan, which is now known as the Great Compromise or the Connecticut Compromise. Connecticut became the fifth state of the new nation when it ratified the Constitution on January 9, 1788.

The True Story of the Slave Ship *La Amistad*

In June 1839, a boat full of slaves from Africa arrived in Cuba. A Spaniard named José Ruiz bought forty-nine adult males from the group for $450 each. Another Spaniard, Pedro Montes, bought four children from another ship. On the night of June 26, Ruiz and Montes and their fifty-three slaves boarded the ship, *La Amistad*, and set out for another part of Cuba where they intended to resell their slaves. On July 1, one of the slaves, Joseph Cinque, freed himself from his wrist chains and iron collar, then began freeing the others. When all the slaves were out of their chains, Cinque led them in a revolt

Joseph Cinque

Cinque (right) and the other rebels from *La Amistad* prepare to return to Africa.

against Ruiz and Montes and the crew. During the rebellion, the ship's captain and cook were killed, along with some of the slaves. The Africans did not know how to steer the ship, so Cinque ordered Ruiz and Montes to sail them back to Africa. During the day, the Spaniards pointed the ship toward Africa, but each night they would change direction, bringing it closer to land. Near the end of August, the ship landed near the eastern end of Long Island, New York, where an American warship found it, escorted the boat and its passengers to New London, Connecticut, then arrested the remaining slaves (more had died since the rebellion).

Mutiny on *La Amistad*

John Quincy Adams

states, abolitionists believed the slaves should be returned to their homeland. Others thought they should be sent back to Cuba to stand trial for murder and piracy. The Northerners hired lawyers to represent the slaves and raised money to pay the legal fee.

After two years and many trials, the case was presented to the United States Supreme Court. Former President John Quincy Adams defended the Africans, saying all men have a right to be free. Cinque and his shipmates had been bought illegally in Africa and imported illegally to Cuba. In January 1842, after their long ordeal, the surviving *Amistad* passengers finally returned to their homeland.

Today you can visit the spot in New Haven where the jail was located and see a statue of Cinque. You also can see a replica of the eighty-five-foot-long wooden schooner docked in Mystic when it is not sailing around other ports of Connecticut.

Although Ruiz and Montes wanted the slaves returned to them, a judge determined that a court should decide the Africans' fate. The slaves were put in jail in New Haven. Because slavery was illegal in Connecticut and the other Northern

Replica of *La Amistad*

Officers of Company 6C from Connecticut, 1864

Preserving the Union

Many Connecticut families owned slaves during colonial times, but independence brought a gradual end to slavery. After March 1, 1784, all children born into slavery in Connecticut were free when they turned twenty-five. By 1848, the last slaves in the state were given their freedom.

In the 1830s and 1840s, though, the Southern and Northern states disagreed about slavery. Connecticut, along with the other Northern states, wanted slavery abolished throughout the nation.

In 1852, a young woman from Connecticut, Harriet Beecher Stowe, wrote a novel called *Uncle Tom's Cabin* about the evils of slavery. The book was immediately successful and strengthened the Northerners' desire to end the practice of slavery. In 1861, with tension mounting between North and South, the Southern states broke away from the Union and declared themselves the Confederate States of America. This was the start of the Civil War.

Factories across Connecticut supplied rifles, rubber boots, gunpowder, and

military transport wagons for the Union war effort. Fifty-five thousand men from the state served in the Union army, and several thousand had been wounded or killed by the time the war ended in 1865.

Industrial Growth

In the years after the Revolutionary War, Connecticut's population exploded. The farmland became so crowded that people began to move north and west, into New York and Ohio. The migration continued throughout the first half of the nineteenth century, with men and women from Connecticut buying land in Michigan, Wisconsin, Minnesota, and eventually farther west.

Connecticut became more industrial during the 1800s, thanks to some of the state's ingenious inventions.

In 1793, Eli Whitney invented a machine called the cotton gin. The machine separated the cotton seeds from the fiber, and suddenly cotton was the most important crop in the Southern United States. (Unfortunately, the cotton gin also contributed to the South's reliance on slaves to harvest the cotton.) In the early 1800s, cotton mills sprouted up all over Connecticut.

Eli Whitney also played an important role in turning Connecticut into a major producer of firearms. He had the idea to standardize gun parts and mass-produce them. Before 1798, when he opened a firearms factory, guns were made one by one by skilled gunmakers. Other manufacturers began using Eli Whitney's methods, Colt and Winchester among them, and the armaments made in the state helped to win the Civil War.

Other inventions from the state include vulcanized rubber (invented by Charles Goodyear), shaving cream, cylinder locks, lollipops, sewing machines, and submarines. More and more mills and factories were built to produce

Slaves working with Eli Whitney's cotton gin

Mass production on an assembly line

these inventions. Once the westward migration began, there were fewer and fewer people left to work in the new industries. Soon immigrants from Europe began to pour into the state and fill out the labor force. Many came from Ireland, Poland, and Italy.

During World War I, Connecticut thrived by producing weapons and other military supplies. After several years of prosperity, from the war years through the mid-1920s, Connecticut fell into a slump during the Great Depression, which began in 1929. Unemployment and poverty soared to record levels until the start of World War II. The European nations needed many of the supplies that Connecticut could provide — weapons, submarines, ships, and communications equipment.

Downtown Hartford

Connecticut Today

Today, Connecticut continues to produce a variety of goods. The state is a leader in fields such as metalworking, electronics, and plastics. Aircraft engines, helicopters, and nuclear submarines are all produced in Connecticut's cities; eggs, apples, corn, and potatoes are the major crops of its farms.

The state is also known for its insurance companies. Beginning in colonial times, insurance companies in Connecticut sold policies to insure ships leaving from its ports in case the goods were damaged. More than one hundred insurance companies have their headquarters in the state, many of them in Hartford, the state capital.

Bridgeport, Connecticut's largest city, is a major seaport, along with the cities of New Haven and New London. These ports handle exports and imports to the state. Many of Connecticut's southern-most towns, such as Darien, Norwalk, and Stamford, are close to New York City, and thousands of people commute by train to work there each day.

As the southernmost state of New England, Connecticut has a thriving tourism industry. In addition to its 618-mile-long shoreline, Connecticut is home to many quaint colonial villages, historic homes, and the unspoiled Connecticut River Valley. The Connecticut River, the longest in New England, runs all the way through the state, passing through Enfield, Windsor, and Hartford in the north and the picturesque towns of Essex, Chester, Old Lyme, and Old Saybrook in the south. The shoreline includes the tiny Thimble Islands as well as beaches, harbors, coves, and bays along the Long Island Sound. The state also contains many state forests and parks for camping, boating, and swimming. It is rich with cultural institutions, including the Wadsworth Atheneum, the oldest public art museum in the country.

Old Saybrook marina

Town along the Connecticut River

Things to Do, Places to See

Dinosaur footprint

Dinosaur State Park

This National Historic Landmark in the town of Rocky Hill has dinosaur tracks from the Jurassic period — more than two million years old. The park also has two huge dioramas showing what the area looked like during the Jurassic and Triassic periods. You can make your own plaster casts of the dinosaur tracks.

Gillette Castle

Gillette Castle State Park

This unusual twenty-four-room castle in Hadlyme was built by a nineteenth-century actor and playwright, William Gillette. Gillette became famous for playing the role of Sherlock Holmes on stage.

Jonathan Trumbull House

Jonathan Trumbull was the first (and only) colonial governor of the state. His home in Lebanon, built around 1735, was a meeting place for leaders of the Revolutionary War. It is now a museum containing many original furnishings from the colonial period.

Jonathan Trumbull House

Keeler Tavern Museum

A popular meeting place for patriots before the Revolutionary War began, this eighteenth-century inn in Ridgefield is famous for the cannonball embedded in one of its corner posts. British troops fired on the inn in 1777 and the cannonball has been there ever since.

Ships in the harbor at Mystic

Mystic Seaport

Mystic Seaport is a re-creation of a nineteenth-century whaling town. Many of the original buildings are still standing, and others were brought from different parts of New England, then reconstructed and restored. Several tall ships are docked at the seaport, including the only surviving wooden whaling ship in the world, built in 1851. The museum houses the largest collection of boats and maritime photography in the world. Nearby is the Mystic Aquarium, with a man-made coral reef, a beluga whale exhibit, and several thousand marine animals on view.

Nathan Hale Homestead

The family house of Revolutionary War hero Nathan Hale was built in 1776 in the town of Coventry. Now a museum, the house holds many original documents, furniture, and family memorabilia. The town of East Haddam has preserved a one-room schoolhouse where Nathan Hale taught between 1773 and 1774.

Nathan Hale Homestead

Mark Twain House

The writer Mark Twain, whose real name was Samuel Clemens, moved to Hartford in 1870 with his wife and family. His two most famous books, *The Adventures of Tom Sawyer* and *The Adventures of Huckleberry Finn*, were both written in the elaborate Victorian mansion that is now a museum.

Mark Twain House

Old State House

This building in Connecticut's capital is the oldest statehouse in the nation. It was here that the first constitution was written (The Fundamental Orders) and two famous trials were held: one about whether it was legal to keep the African slaves from the ship *La Amistad* in the New World after they revolted and landed near Connecticut's shores; the other about a woman named Prudence Crandall, a teacher who opened a school for black girls when the state declared it was illegal.

Old State House

Peabody Museum of Natural History

One of several museums and libraries on the campus of Yale University in New Haven, the Peabody Museum contains exhibits of dinosaur fossils, wildlife dioramas, and Native American cultures. Other museums on the Ivy League campus include the Yale Center for British Art and the Yale University Art Gallery, the oldest university art museum in the nation.

Poster from P. T. Barnum's Greatest Show on Earth

P. T. Barnum Museum

Built in 1893 in Bridgeport just two years after the death of the founder of the Barnum & Bailey Circus, the museum houses exhibits and mementos of P. T. Barnum, Tom Thumb, and Jenny Lind, a famous singer known as "the Swedish Nightingale." Clothes worn by tiny Tom Thumb, a man only twenty-eight-inches tall, are displayed, along with a hand-carved miniature circus, clown props, and other circus memorabilia.

P. T. Barnum Museum

16th-century Pequot village walk-through diorama

Mashantucket Pequot Museum

In this museum, which houses exhibits about the Native American and natural history of southern New England, fifty-one life-size figures populate a half-acre 1550 Pequot village, depicting everyday activities of the tribe. You can walk through the village, see several different films about the exhibits, and enter a glacial crevasse created 18,000 years ago.

Prison ruins

Old New-Gate Prison and Copper Mine

The prison building in East Granby (built in 1773) was Connecticut's first colonial prison and held many captured British soldiers during the Revolutionary War. The prisoners were forced to work in the copper mine during the day before being chained to the walls for the night. You can walk through the tunnels of the prison, two hundred feet underground, and still see the rusting chains.

Submarine Museum

U.S.S. Nautilus and Submarine Museum

The world's first nuclear-powered submarine, the U.S.S. *Nautilus,* was launched from the town of Groton in 1954. Today you can board the submarine, explore the control room, and take in the underwater view from a periscope. You can also learn the history of submarines.

Famous People from Connecticut

Phineas Taylor (P. T.) Barnum (1810–1891)

American showman P. T. Barnum, born in Bethel, began his career by staging unusual exhibitions, such as introducing General Tom Thumb and Siamese twins Chang and Eng. In 1871, he launched his traveling circus, "The Greatest Show on Earth." Ten years later, he merged his circus with one run by James Anthony Bailey, and soon the Barnum & Bailey Circus became world famous.

John Brown (1800–1859)

Born in Torrington, the famous abolitionist John Brown led a raid on Harpers Ferry, Virginia, on October 16, 1859, hoping to free slaves by armed force, then provide refuge for them. He was able to take over the town, but soon he and his band of supporters were surrounded by the local militia and the U.S. Marines, and a violent battle ensued. Ten of Brown's men were killed, and he was wounded and captured. At his trial, he was found guilty of treason and murder and was sentenced to be hanged.

Glenn Close (1947–   )

Actress Glenn Close, born in Greenwich, has starred in Broadway shows, major films, and television movies. She has won several Tony Awards and has been nominated many times for Academy Awards. Her work includes roles in *The Big Chill* and *Sarah, Plain and Tall*. She played the villain Cruella De Vil in *101 Dalmations*.

Ella Grasso (1919–1981)

Politician Ella Grasso was born in Windsor Locks to Italian immigrant parents. She started out in state politics, first as a member of the Connecticut House of Representatives and then as the state's Secretary of State. Next she was elected to Congress, and finally to the office of governor of Connecticut, the first woman in the nation to win in her own right. All previous women governors had taken over the position from someone else. Ella Grasso never lost an election and was an immensely popular governor.

Nathan Hale (1755–1776)

Coventry native Nathan Hale was a teacher and patriot who served as a spy for George Washington in 1776. He was captured and hanged by the British. He is the official state hero of Connecticut and known for his famous last words: "I only regret that I have but one life to lose for my country."

Katharine Hepburn (1907–)

Born in Hartford, Katharine Hepburn is one of America's most famous actresses. She has received twelve nominations for Academy Awards and won four for best actress. Some of her best-known films are *The Philadelphia Story*, *Adam's Rib*, and *Guess Who's Coming to Dinner*.

Charles Ives (1874–1954)

Charles Ives, from Danbury, wrote his first musical compositions when he was just a boy. He studied music at Yale Universty, then moved to New York City, where he worked in the insurance business. Ives continued to write experimental music, although it was rarely performed. Eventually other musicians began to discover and perform his unconventional pieces. His works include four symphonies, the third of which was awarded a Pulitzer Prize forty years after he wrote it.

Ralph Nader (1934–)

Born in the town of Winsted, lawyer, consumer advocate, and politician Ralph Nader became famous nationally with his book *Unsafe at Any Speed*, published in 1965. The book made it clear to the American public that many automobiles were not manufactured or designed with passengers' safety in mind. Today, all cars must pass certain government safety tests. Nader also promoted other issues of public concern, including pollution, nuclear energy, and waste of government funds.

Frederick Law Olmstead (1822–1903)

Hartford native Frederick Law Olmstead is America's most famous landscape architect. Along with Calvert Vaux, he designed New York City's Central Park and Riverside Park. He also designed the grounds of the Capitol in Washington, D.C. Olmstead was one of the first landscape architects in America to make use of the land's natural features, incorporating boulders, bodies of water, and existing paths into his designs.

Eugene O'Neill (1888–1953)

Though born in New York City, playwright Eugene O'Neill spent his childhood summers in New London at his family's home, Monte Cristo Cottage. Considered one of the greatest playwrights of the twentieth century, O'Neill wrote such realistic family dramas as *Long Day's Journey into Night* and *A Moon for the Misbegotten*. He won the Pulitzer Prize four times and was awarded the Nobel Prize in literature in 1936.

Harriet Beecher Stowe (1811–1896)

Harriet Beecher Stowe's antislavery novel, *Uncle Tom's Cabin*, was published in 1852, nine years before the Civil War started. Born in Litchfield, Harriet later moved to Ohio, where she observed firsthand how poorly slaves were treated. Her book helped spread antislavery feelings in the North, and some people think it was a factor in the start of the Civil War. The house in Hartford where she spent the last years of her life is now a museum.

Noah Webster (1758–1843)

A native of Hartford, Noah Webster compiled and published the first major American dictionary in 1828 after twenty-five years of research. He also wrote history and spelling textbooks. You can visit the farmhouse where he was born and see what life was like in the eighteenth and nineteenth centuries.

Eli Whitney (1765–1825)

Eli Whitney is best known as the inventor of the cotton gin, although he also invented a way to mass-produce standard and interchangeable parts for firearms. He was born in Massachusetts but spent all of his adult life in Connecticut after attending Yale University. His factory, just outside of New Haven in the town of Hamden, is open to visitors.